W9-CVA-894

You will also enjoy

CANVAS WORK SIMPLIFIED

More than any other form of embroidery, Canvas Work is restful, absorbing and creative. No expensive equipment or materials are needed, and there are no complicated techniques. All that is required are a few skeins of wool, a tapestry needle, and a piece of canvas.

Half cross stitch is the only stitch used for all the designs in this book. It can be mastered in a matter of minutes and has been chosen because of its versatility and the speed with which it can be worked. For the more experienced embroiderer and for those wishing to experiment, many different stitches are possible, and a corresponding diversity of results achieved.

24 plates in full colour, plus photographs, sketches and diagrams, show delightful items of canvas work for the home, to give as presents, and for personal use. Detailed instructions are provided for making belts, hair bands, greetings cards, frames to pictures, pincushions, boxes and purses. There are also sections on how to adapt designs for canvas work, lettering, fashion accessories, and inspiration for design.

Joan Nicholson is a well-known embroiderer and designer.

Patchwork Simplified

Patchwork Simplified

Alice Timmins

Arco Publishing Company, Inc
New York

Published by Arco Publishing Company, Inc.
219 Park Avenue South, New York, N.Y. 10003

Copyright © 1973 by Alice Timmins

All rights reserved

Library of Congress Catalog Card Number 73-79197
ISBN 0 668 03321 5

Printed in Great Britain

26873

Contents

Acknowledgment

I wish to thank all those who have given me permission to use photographs of their work in this book.

I am grateful also to Harry Timmins, who took most of the photographs, to Anne Butler, Head of Embroidery School, Faculty of Art and Design, Manchester Polytechnic, to Thelma M Nye, of Batsfords, and to Catherine Timmins, who typed the manuscript.

Chorley, Lancashire   AT

Sources of ideas

The most obvious sources of ideas for patchwork are books and exhibitions. A number of books on the subject are available, and a study of these can be rewarding. But books on painting, sculpture, graphics, printing, mosaics, or any art form may also hold the beginning of an idea which could lead to fresh and original design. Many such books can be found in public libraries. In the same way, exhibitions of both modern and traditional art and crafts could be a source of inspiration, and no opportunity to see different types of work both at home and abroad should be missed.

But individuality in patchwork depends to a large extent on the ability to recognise possibilities for design in the colours and patterns to be seen every day. An arrangement of fields on a hillside is a common sight; groups of buildings, fun fairs, patterns of sunlight on leaves, flowers in parks and gardens, stones and rocks, or assemblies of people can often spark off an idea. Many churches, cathedrals, and important buildings have stained glass windows of splendid colour, either subtle and sombre or vibrant and glowing. Shafts of light or spotlights often cause dramatic changes of tone and hue.

Again, a display of dress or furnishing fabrics in a shop, or a pile of 'fents' on a market stall, or even the colours on a particular piece of fabric may suggest an idea for patchwork.

The best results however, may not be achieved if these things are copied in a naturalistic way. Some aspect of colour or pattern should be selected and a design developed from this.

This book contains photographs and drawings of articles which would be attractive to wear or use in the home, but they are only suggestions, and many variations, using different colours and different templates are possible. Most of these ideas are based on traditional work of some type; results which are in keeping with today's attitudes can be achieved by adapting old techniques and using them with modern fabrics in an adventurous way. The sewing machine makes possible new and speedier ways of joining patches and some possibilities are suggested which could be developed.

It will be found that the greater the involvement, the stronger the flow of ideas will become.

Equipment

Needles
These should be as fine as can be used successfully. The size should be related to the thickness of the thread.

Threads
Pure silk for silk fabrics.
Nylon thread for fabrics from man-made fibres.
Cotton for other fabrics, no. 40 to 100 according to the skill and eyesight of the worker. Black should be used for sewing dark patches together and white for light ones. When sewing light patches to dark ones, black cotton seems to show least.
Mercerised cotton for machine sewing.
Tacking cotton (basting thread).

Scissors
Sharp pair for fabrics.
Old pair for paper.

Paper
Strong paper such as that used for large heavy envelopes is good for beginners. Skilled workers find fairly thin notepaper of good quality most suitable. Thin white cardboard is only used for projects such as mobiles when it must be left in.

Vilene or Pellon
Heavy weight 274
This is good for bags, boxes and panels instead of paper patterns as it can be left in as part of the padding or backing.

Pins
Fine steel or brass.

Thimble
This is necessary for speedy and rhythmic work.

Templates
See pages 11 to 13.

Fabrics

Most fabrics can be used for patchwork provided that they do not stretch or fray easily.

The larger the collection of both plain and patterned fabrics, the richer in colour and texture the results will be. The following materials are suitable:

Cotton: smooth or textured, dull or shiny, eg piqué, twill, sateen, strawcloth, cotton velvet, towelling, fabrics with slub weaves

Linen may be combined with cotton of similar weight

Silk and **velvet** may be used together

Felt

Wool and wool and cotton mixtures

Fabrics containing lurex

Fabrics from man-made fibres. Transparent ones will need a backing of similar fabric

Rayons which stretch and fraz easily should be avoided.

NOTE
The different fabrics used in one piece of work should be of similar weight.

All creases should be pressed out before the patches are cut.

It is advisable to wash small cuttings if there is any doubt about the fastness of the dyes.

Pieces of old garments may be used if not weakened by wear or many washings.

Fabrics with naturalistic floral patterns and those with geometrical ones do not combine well.

Templates

Templates must be completely accurate. They may be bought from the firms listed on page 96, but they can be made as shown in the diagrams on pages 12 and 13.

Metal, *Perspex*, *Plexiglass*, acetate or cardboard may be used. The latter is not suitable for large projects as the edges tend to wear away with the action of the scissors when the paper patterns are cut.

Metals can be cut with special shears, and cardboard with a sharp handicraft knife. A metal ruler, protractor, compasses and a set square are necessary.

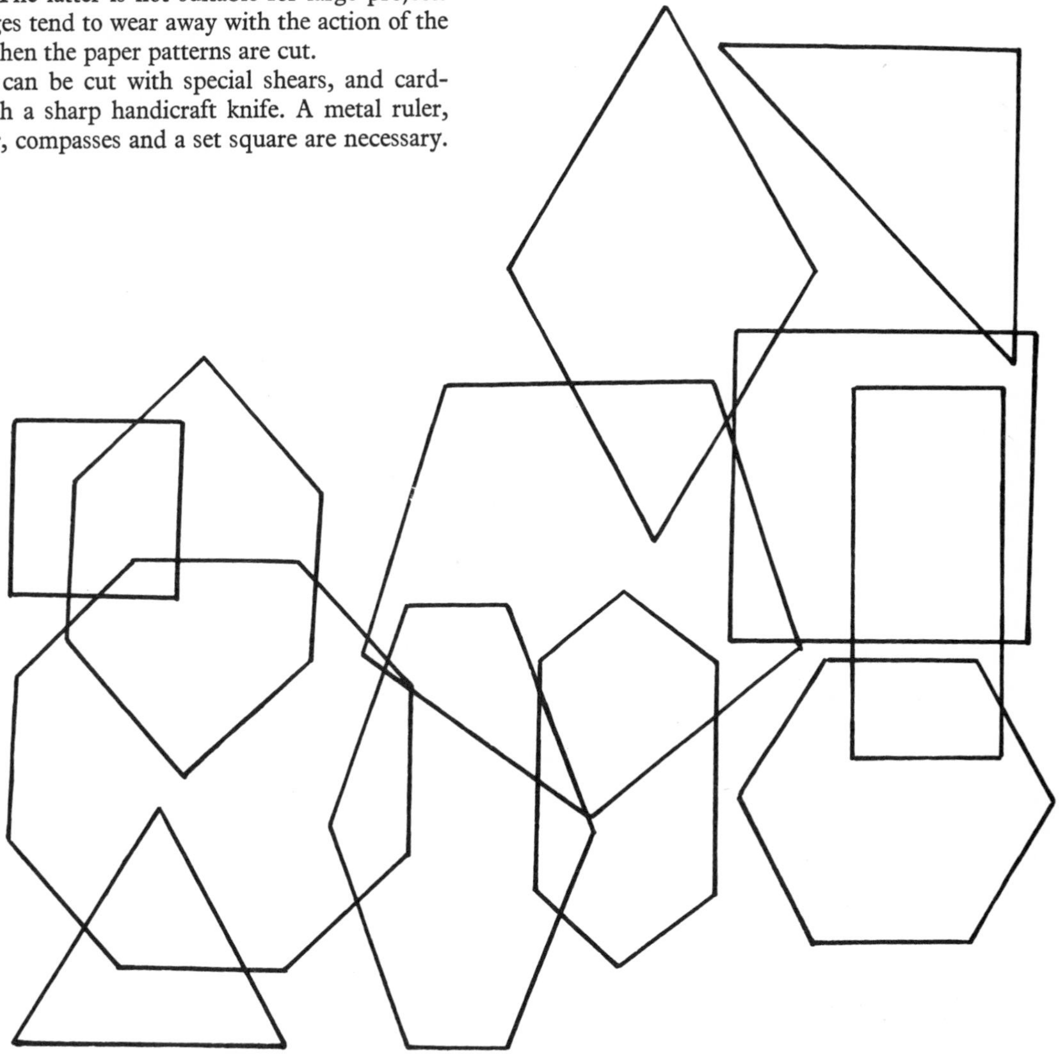

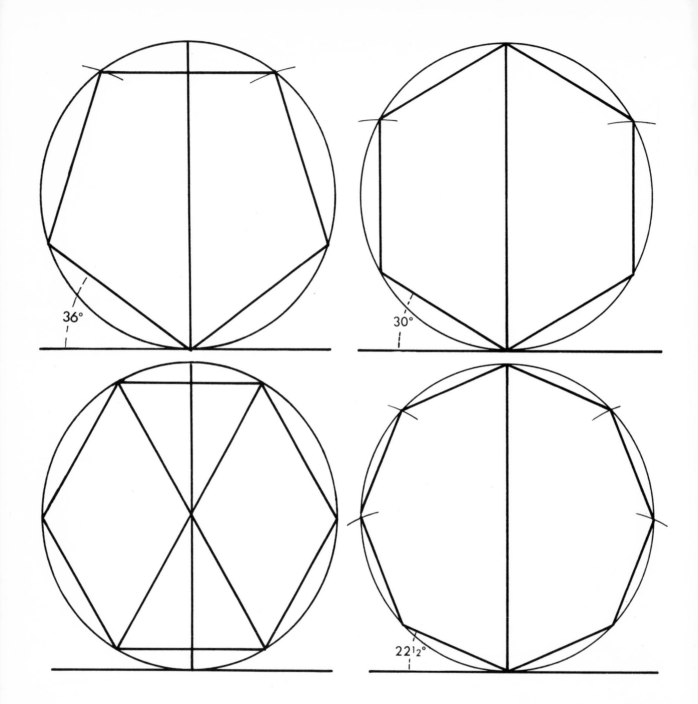

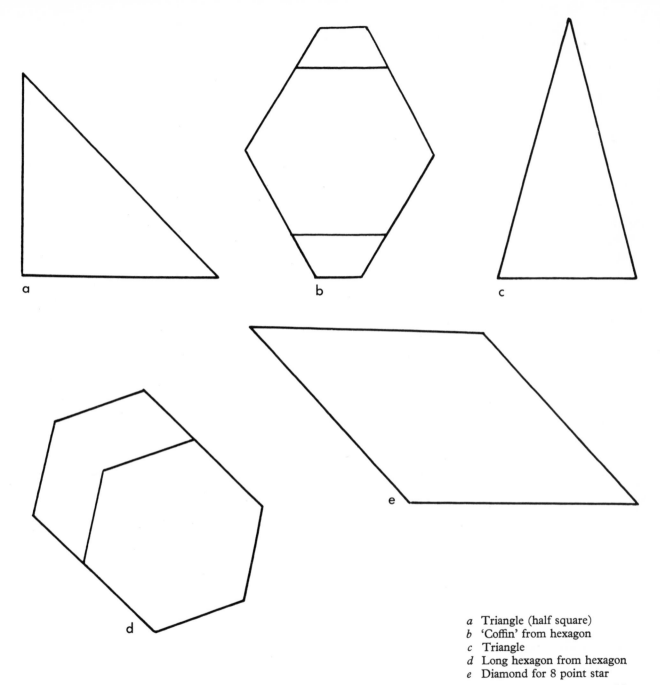

a Triangle (half square)
b 'Coffin' from hexagon
c Triangle
d Long hexagon from hexagon
e Diamond for 8 point star

13

Paper patterns

Paper patterns are cut with the templates held firmly on the paper and with the scissor blades touching the edge of the template as they cut around it. They must be accurate.

It is good practice to cut paper patterns from the coloured and black and white pages of old magazines. These can be used to make decorative paper patch-work panels which made colourful classroom decorations.

Paper patterns, if taken out carefully, may be used several times.

Acetate can also be used to give attractive results.

Acetate patchwork by Marjorie Timmins. Note the marks made by the adhesive which adds interest to the work

Paper patchwork

Paper patchwork by Marjorie Timmins

Fabric patches

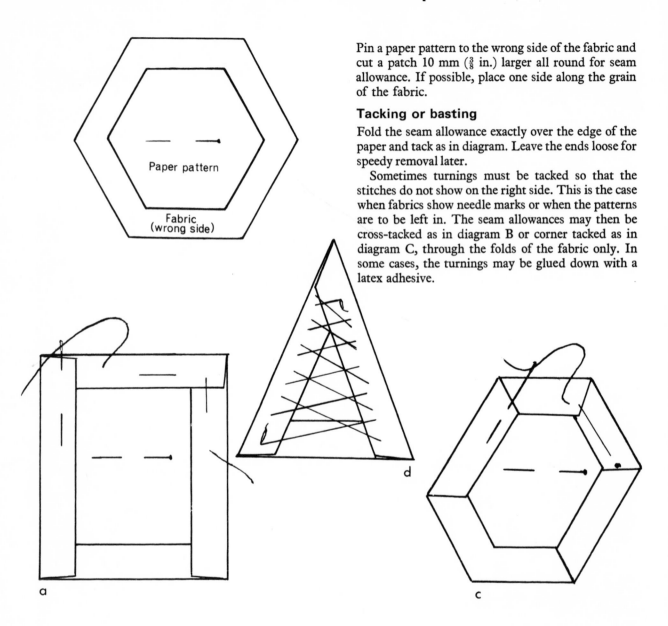

Paper pattern

Fabric
(wrong side)

a

c

d

Pin a paper pattern to the wrong side of the fabric and cut a patch 10 mm ($\frac{3}{8}$ in.) larger all round for seam allowance. If possible, place one side along the grain of the fabric.

Tacking or basting

Fold the seam allowance exactly over the edge of the paper and tack as in diagram. Leave the ends loose for speedy removal later.

Sometimes turnings must be tacked so that the stitches do not show on the right side. This is the case when fabrics show needle marks or when the patterns are to be left in. The seam allowances may then be cross-tacked as in diagram B or corner tacked as in diagram C, through the folds of the fabric only. In some cases, the turnings may be glued down with a latex adhesive.

Three stages in covering a diamond paper pattern

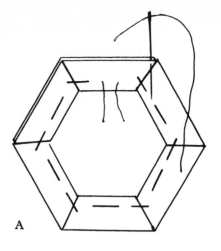

A

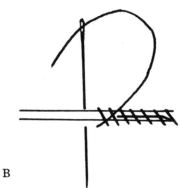

B

Seaming

Place two patches with right sides together. Take the first stitch through the front patch only, as near to the corner as possible as in diagram A.

Lay the end of the cotton along the top of the patches and seam over it from right to left, as in diagram B.

To fasten off, work backwards for 4 stitches as in diagram C.

Sometimes several patches can be joined without fastening off.

When making a diamond star, seam from A to B and fasten off each time. This eases the fabric to the centre and helps to prevent leaving a hole. See diagram D.

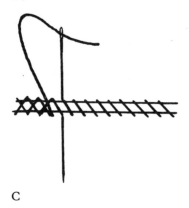

C

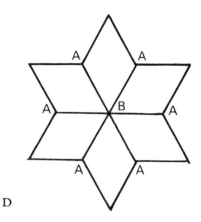

D

Finishing off

When all the patches are sewn together, press on the wrong side

This helps to hold the turnings in place.

Take out tackings and papers.

Press on the right side under a slightly damp cloth, stretching the patchwork gently at the same time. It is then ready for making up.

If the patchwork is pressed in this way there should be no ironing difficulties in subsequent launderings.

Hand-sewn patchwork should *never* be washed before making up, as it might lose its shape, but it may be necessary to wash some machine-made types.

Advice to beginners

Having read the previous chapters, collected equipment and materials, and decided on the article to be made, a number of patches can now be prepared.

Place these patches on a large sheet of paper or a cork mat, and try different arrangements (see page 23) keeping in mind the shape of the finished article, for the pattern created with the patches must have some relation to this.

Look at the result in a half light so as to make sure that the tones as well as the colours are well placed. Perhaps one patch is too light or too dark and should be replaced with one of the right tone.

View it again at a distance in full light, and if it is satisfactory, pin the patches down. This should not be done if pin marks will show, in which case the patchwork could be kept on a tray or board. It is important not to disturb the pattern at this stage.

The patches can then be sewn together, making sure that the stitches are taken to the very ends of the seams – sometimes several patches can be joined using the same length of thread.

The making up of the article should be carefully done, as the finish can enhance or spoil a piece of work.

Care of patchwork

It is not wise to expose patchwork to strong sunlight, which could caues colours to fade.

Articles in daily use should not be allowed to become very soiled before action is taken.

Patchwork may be washed by hand, using a mild soap, but if several different fabrics are used, it should be dry-cleaned.

Design

Colour, tone and texture, are important aspects of design in patchwork.

Colour

The colours chosen may be influenced by personal preferences: dark and subtle, pale and delicate, or vibrant and glowing hues have appeal for different temperaments.

They may be selected to harmonize quietly or contrast dramatically with the colour scheme of a room. In, for example, a cushion or a panel for a room with cold colours, a combination of reds, orange and purples could add warmth and contrast, while cool greens and blues might be pleasant and restful in the same room, especially if it is a sunny one.

In the article made, colours which harmonize with each other, (eg blue and green), produce a calm and restful design, but if contrasting ones are used, (eg red and green of the same value) a lively and vibrant effect can be achieved.

The proportions of the colours used are also important. If equal amounts of two different colours are used, there may be an unresolved conflict between them, and the result may not be pleasing.

A larger amount of one colour than of the other will give a more acceptable design.

Tone

Tone should always be kept in mind in patchwork, and must be considered as much as the hues of the fabrics. The tone of a colour is its lightness or darkness; for example pale blue is lighter in tone than dark blue. Some colours, too, are in their pure form lighter than others, and a study of the colour circle will show this. Mixed colours, such as grey, can be dark or light, and may appear to be of the same tone as such different hues as yellow or purple. If the tone values in a piece of patchwork are difficult to distinguish from each other, the design should be looked at in a dim light, or through dark glasses, or with the eyes half closed. The colours will then be less evident and may disappear altogether, leaving the different tones of the patches showing clearly.

When the only fabrics available are of very many different hues, it is best to make a design using tone values only. A light patch could be surrounded by darker ones of any colour and these in turn could have much darker patches around them. Many different arrangements could be made.

There will obviously be slight differences of tone in the reds, greens, browns, etc, used, but this will add sparkle to the design. Strong tonal contrasts will produce a more striking effect than subtle ones, see facing page. The latter can be used if a restful type of design is needed.

Against the Evil Eye Patches made with various red fabrics on a red background, incorporating Israeli beads

Medal Silver lurex and shocking pink ribbons with purple and red stripes on a dark purple background with black stripes

Texture

This can add vitality to many patchwork designs which might otherwise be dull. It is well worth while to collect as many fabrics as possible which are of interesting texture.

It is possible to make good designs in patchwork by using

(a) All plain fabrics
(b) All patterned fabrics
(c) A mixture of these two.

A design using all plain fabrics of almost the same colour can have much more vitality if they are of different types (shiny and dull silks and cottons, velvets, corduroys and tweeds).

These mixed materials are particularly suited for panels, where the necessity for dry cleaning rarely occurs, see page 84. This is not the case for articles in daily use which are likely to become soiled fairly quickly, as they will not wash well. If however, the plain fabrics available are of various colours, a satisfactory design can be made if the colours and tones are harmonised or contrasted.

If all patterned fabrics are used, variations of colour, tone and type of print in the different patches are important in the design. Some patches with a small pattern would combine well with others of a bolder type, or some paler ones with darker ones, taking care to preserve the identity of each patch.

Uninteresting areas in a design will often result if a length of material is cut up and the pieces sewn together again. Sometimes this may be avoided if both right and wrong sides are used, or in some cases if the patches are placed in such a way that the play of light on them alters their tone slightly.

A number of pieces of fabric of different types may be dyed together and the inevitable small differences which are bound to appear will be of advantage. In nature, these variations are to be seen in the bark and leaves of a tree, pebbles on a beach and even in a single flower. It could be a revelation to examine such things and to note how many colours, tones and textures are to be seen.

It is a mistake to rely too much on the patterns printed on or woven into the fabrics used, and to cut out motifs in a way which wastes the material. Although these are plentiful today and the need for thrift is not urgent, it should be remembered that the origin of patchwork lies in economy. Much traditional work owes its charm and vitality to the fact that every scrap of fabric was used.

By cutting motifs so that they lie in the same place in each patch, and then arranging these in a precise and symmetrical way, a monotonous, over-contrived and even 'chocolate box' effect will, in most cases, be achieved. If motifs are cut out, they should be used in an individual and dramatic way..

When the cut out motifs are carefully arranged so that the pattern on one appears to continue on the next, the construction of the patchwork is

Almost identical patches have been used in each sampler. Variations in the positions of the dark and light ones have created three different designs

23

hidden, and this is not a desirable result in any craft. Each patch should have its individual value. Its shape should be clearly discernable, while at the same time it should have its own part to play in the finished design.

Cushion top being made by Marjorie Timmins. 25 mm (1 in.) squares, chiefly in reds and pinks

PATCHWORK USING TRADITIONAL TECHNIQUES

In traditional work, designs were sometimes made by using a series of borders sewn together. Often strips of plain materials were used to separate them. Such designs could be used today with good effect for cushions, bedcovers, and wallhangings

Pincushions

A pincushion, if large and dramatic enough in colour, adds interest to any room.

All its sides may be of patchwork or it may have a plain back.

Most pincushions are stuffed with tightly packed sheepswool or finely cut up knitting wool. Sawdust, however, or dried washed tea leaves in a bag of suitable size may be used. The insertion of thin card will make a flat base.

Finishing

The edges may be seamed together, or piped (see page 46) or finished with a cord.

When joining the side seams, leave a gap about 5 cm (2 in.) long. Remove papers and tack around this opening. Turn right side out, stuff, and close the opening with ladder stitch, as shown in the diagrams.

Ladder stitch – the edges are pulled together

Needlecase

Both back and front are patchwork, but the back could be plain. *Vilene* or paper may be used for patterns which are left in.

Method

1 Make patchwork (25 mm (1 in.) square patches)
2 Open out the turnings round three sides.
3 Cover a strip of *Vilene* or thin card 15 mm x 12.7 cm ($\frac{1}{2}$ in. x 5 in.) with fabric and seam this on the wrong side to the fourth sides of the back and front to form a hinge.
4 Stretch patchwork over pieces of thin card 12.7 cm x 12.7 cm (5 in. x 5 in.) fold turnings over and stick them down.
5 Line with suitable fabric, making pockets first.
6 Cut felt or flannel about 22.8 cm x 10 cm (9 in. x 4 in.) with pinking shears and sew to hinge.
7 A button and buttonhole loop may be added. See also 'Rolled button', page 46.

Glasses case

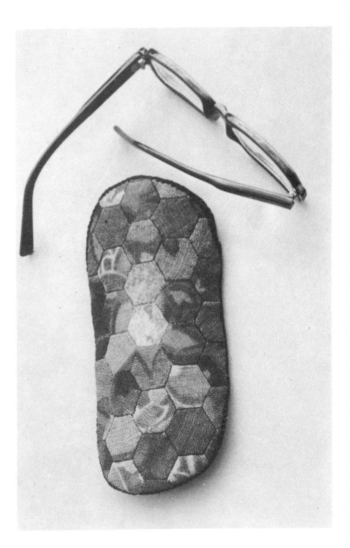

Glasses case made by Jessie Doodson. 13 mm ($\frac{1}{2}$ in.) hexagons in rich reds, greens and blues. The front is 3 mm ($\frac{1}{8}$ in.) wider than the back. Thin card is used for stiffening.

Place mats

Place mats can be made in different sizes and shapes
– square, oblong, hexagonal or triangular, and may,
or may not, be small enough to be covered entirely
by the plates used.

Some place mats are made entirely of patchwork,
while others have an area of plain fabric.

Ideas for place mats: square, hexagons, oblongs and Dresden plate

Place mat in octagons and 15 mm (½ in.) squares

Back view of place mat showing a way of finishing the edges. A row of patches is seamed to the edge patches of the front of the mat (right sides together). The papers are removed and these extra patches are turned over to the lining, to which they are hemmed

Place mat 30.5 cm x 40.5 cm (12 in. x 16 in.). Floral design in white patchwork on a blue and white striped fabric. Stems are machine stitched in white. The edges are bound with white cotton bias strip

Hot dish holder

1 Cut piece of fabric 117.8 cm x 35.6 cm (44 in. x 14 in.)
2 Make two hexagon flowers or diamond stars in patchwork. Remove papers and re-tack outside folds.
3 Pin and tack them in place on right side as shown in the diagram, and hem them down.
4 Machine or attach in some way squares of thick soft fabric on wrong side.
5 Fold AB over to CD (right sides together) and machine round 15 mm ($\frac{1}{2}$ in.) from edge, leaving an opening. Turn right side out and close opening.
6 Fold ends over on dotted line and join at sides to form a bag at each end.

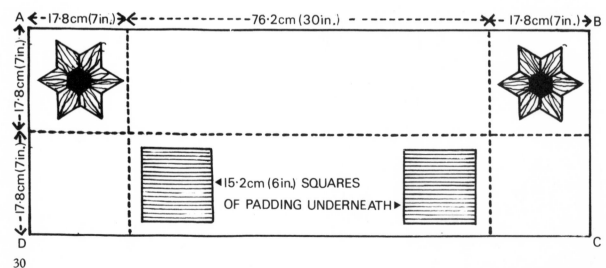

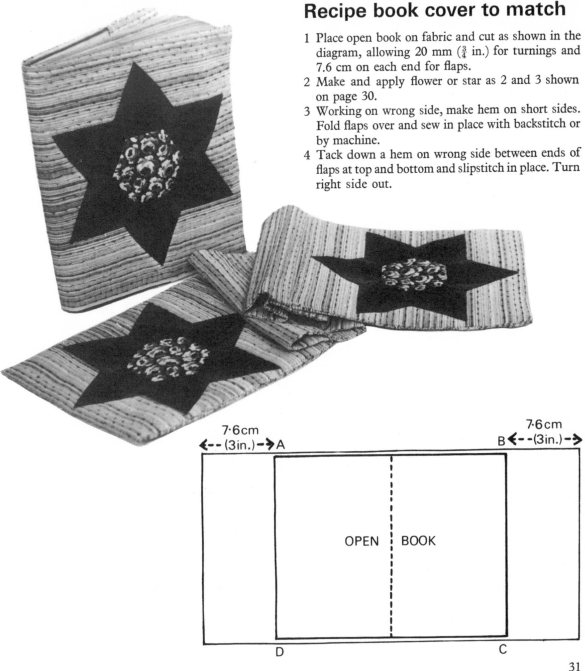

Recipe book cover to match

1 Place open book on fabric and cut as shown in the diagram, allowing 20 mm ($\frac{3}{4}$ in.) for turnings and 7.6 cm on each end for flaps.
2 Make and apply flower or star as 2 and 3 shown on page 30.
3 Working on wrong side, make hem on short sides. Fold flaps over and sew in place with backstitch or by machine.
4 Tack down a hem on wrong side between ends of flaps at top and bottom and slipstitch in place. Turn right side out.

7·6 cm
←‑‑(3in.)‑→A

7·6 cm
B ←‑‑(3in.)‑→

OPEN ⦙ BOOK

D   C

Tea cosy with matching egg cosy

5 cm (2 in.) diamond template.

Made from cottons in clear bright pinks and greens, with touches of white and yellow, this would make a cheerful set for a breakfast tray.

Egg cosy

1 Cover and join six patches and two half patches.
2 Join AC to BD, CE to DF and EG to FH, thus forming a tube.

3 Fold this flat, right side inside, and seam the top patches together from A to I and I to J. Remove tackings and papers and press.
4 Make up a lining to fit and hem it to inside turnings at base. Secure with a few stitches at I.

Tea cosy

This is made in the same way, but with 41 patches and 6 half patches.

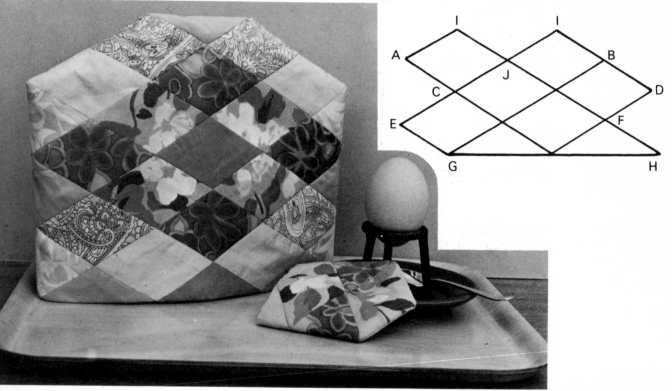

Coffee pot cosy, hand made by Sylvia Murdock ▶
The design was first drawn on paper. Method is described on page 91
Reproduced by courtesy of *Woman* magazine

Caterpillar

Hexagonal template

This toy can be sewn by hand or machine and can have any number of sections of any size.

Method

By hand

1 Prepare patches (two for each section).
2 Seam each pair together on wrong side, leaving one side open.
3 Remove tackings and papers, and re-tack round open sides without disturbing fold, as shown in the diagram on page 26.
4 Turn right side out and stuff each section – (cut up nylon stockings are suitable).
5 Close opening with ladder stitch.

By machine

1 Cut required number of hexagons in fabric, allowing turnings.
2 Place template on wrong side of the top patches, and mark round in pencil or tailor's chalk.
3 Place the other patches under these, right sides together and on the lines drawn, machine round five sides.
4 Complete as for hand sewing method.

Joining the sections

For strength, two rows of stitching, first seaming, then ladder stitch, are advisable. Several stitches, one over the other, at each end, will also help.

A snake can be made from diamond shaped patches sewn into a long tube, with a head added.

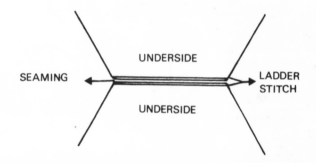

Snake

A snake can be made from diamond shaped patches sewn into a long tube, with a head added.

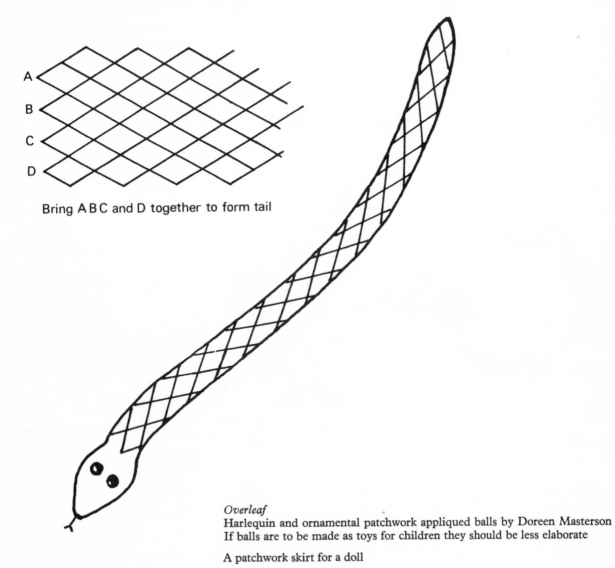

Bring A B C and D together to form tail

Overleaf
Harlequin and ornamental patchwork appliqued balls by Doreen Masterson
If balls are to be made as toys for children they should be less elaborate

A patchwork skirt for a doll

Ball

If fabric is used, prepare 24Y and 12Z patches in the traditional way. Felt can be seamed on the wrong side, or stitched on the right side with running stitches close to the edge.

Method

1 Join 2 Y patches from A to C and B to C, leaving opening.
2 Join a Z patch to this from A to B, both sides, making a bag. Turn right side out.
3 Stuff and close opening with ladder stitch.
4 Make three of these and seam them together from C to A and C to B.
5 Make four similar sets of three, and place all sets together with each C in the centre of the ball.
6 Stitch firmly where A and B points meet. Button-hole bars or 'spider's webs' may be worked at these points to give added strength.

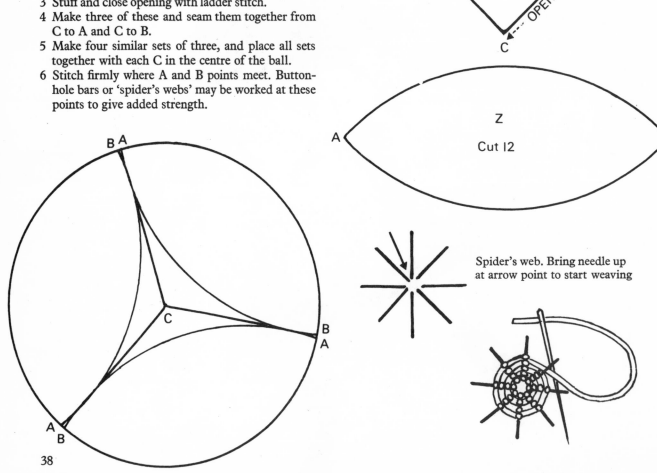

Spider's web. Bring needle up at arrow point to start weaving

Lavender bags

Ball made by Mona Hughes

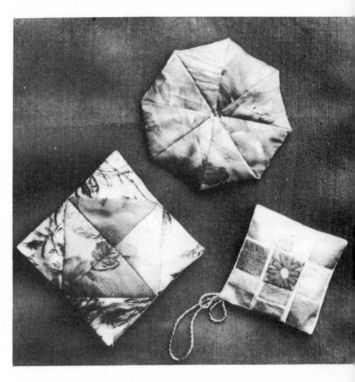

Lavender bags by Alice Timmins
Right Small fabric squares of white nylon fabric, printed in silver and gold. Centre square is pink, green and mauve
Top Triangles of pure silk with sequin in centre
Left Right-angled triangles of pure silk in pinks and blues

Overleaf
Pincushions, designed and hand made by Alice Timmins
Right Octagon with 15 mm ($\frac{1}{2}$ in.) squares
Centre Cube based on 5 cm (2 in.) squares
Left 25 mm (1 in.) squares

An asymmetrical design.
A first attempt at patchwork by Wendy Young

Mobile

Method

1 For each unit cut 4 diamond shapes in thin strong card.
2 Score each one across the shortest diagonal, using metal ruler and knife, and making a shallow cut which must go only half way through the card.
3 Cover each set of 4 cards with fabric, sticking down the turnings over to the wrong side.
4 Bend cards over on scored lines, and ladder stitch or oversew each set of 4 together.
5 Join units with varying lengths of invisible nylon thread.

Christmas tree ornament

This is made in the same way as each unit of the mobile. Decorations are added, together with a loop at the top.

Cushions

Both back and front may be of patchwork, but often the back is a piece of plain fabric of a suitable colour.

Method of making up

1 Cut fabric for back exactly the same size as patchwork top when the edge turnings are opened out.
2 Check to see that opposite sides are equal.
3 Sew up in one of the following ways:
Seam back and front together on wrong side, leaving an opening, OR open out edge turnings and backstitch or machine stitch round 10 mm ($\frac{3}{8}$ in.) from edge, OR insert a piping cord. See diagrams on page 46.

The cushion pad should always be slightly larger than the cover.

An edging of hand made or bought cord, or a fringe, may sometimes improve the design.

A permanent opening with buttons and loops or press studs, a zip fastener, or *Velcro*, can be used to complete the cushion.

Permanent opening for cushion

Cut a straight strip of fabric about 5 cm (2 in.) wide and twice the length of the opening, plus 20 mm ($\frac{3}{4}$ in.).

Pin this along both sides of the opening with the right sides together (diagram A).

Join the ends of the strip, and sew it to the opening 10 mm ($\frac{3}{8}$ in.) from the edge.

Turn over the strip to the wrong side, make a single turning and hem down (diagram B). No stitches should show on the right side.

Fold the strip over to the inside. The dotted lines on diagram C show how it fits.

Sew on buttons and loops.

Square button 15mm ($\frac{1}{2}$in.)

Cut two pieces of heavy weight *Vilene* (*Pellon*) or other stiffening material 15 mm ($\frac{1}{2}$ in.) square. Cover each with a piece of fabric 25 mm (1 in.) square (diagram D).

Put the two together with turnings inside and ladder stitch or seam together.

Sew on with shank (diagram E).

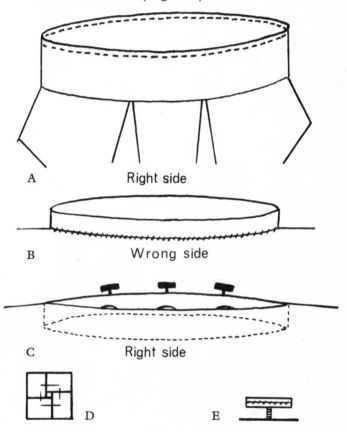

A   Right side

B   Wrong side

C   Right side

D

E

Overleaf   Cushion of long hexagonal patches, hand made by Annie Barnes. It has a zip fastener

Floor cushion, 7.6 cm (30 in.), square machine made by Marjorie Timmins Long narrow strips of patterned corduroy on a calico background are joined with zigzag stitches (method 3 see page 91). Some sections have joins placed horizontally, some vertically

Rolled button

Rolled button 15 mm ($\frac{1}{2}$ in.) wide.
Cut a strip of fabric 25 mm (1 in.) wide and about
12.7 cm (5 in.) long. Turn the long sides over to the
middle and catch together. Roll up very tightly from
one end; make a single fold and hem this down. Sew
on with a shank.

Piping a cushion

Tack piping cord (pre-shrunk by washing) inside
crossway strip about 3.8 cm (1$\frac{1}{2}$ in.) wide (diagram A).

Starting in the middle of one side, place the raw
edges of this piping along the raw edges of the cushion
top, and pin. Leave about 7.6 cm (3 in.) free at the
beginning and end for joining.

To join, cut the cord to the exact length needed and
glue the ends together with a latex adhesive. Fold the
ends of the bias strip so that the edges meet, pin
press and sew together on the crease made (diagram
B).

Finish pinning in the piping, check to make sure
that opposite sides are equal and tack all round. Snip
the raw edges of the piping at each corner close to
the stitches.

Tack on the piece for the back of the cushion
(diagram C shows section), and backstitch or machine
close to cord. Leave an opening for inserting pad.

For a round cushion, the piping must be snipped
all the way round.

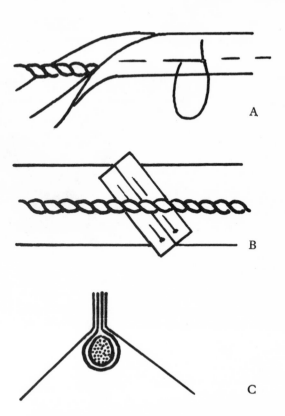

A

B

C

Designs for cushions
Left Lighter square patches in orange, pinks and purple. Darker border
patches in browns and purples
Right 'Church window' patches in reds, pinks, yellows and white with darker
turquoise and olive green
Below Olive greens, browns and reds, with some brighter greens

Overleaf Diamond panel by Alice Timmins. Design drawn out on paper and sections
covered with fabric. Hand sewn

One of a series of panels made for a patchwork project by second year students.
See also pages 82 and 83

47

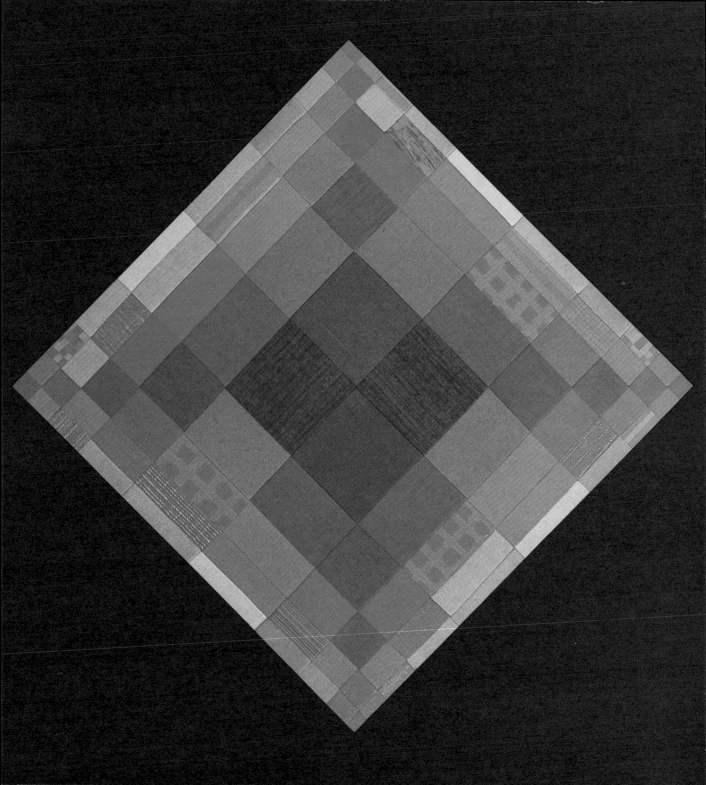

Triangles of different heights but with similar bases combined in one piece of work. Templates can be cut from strong card.

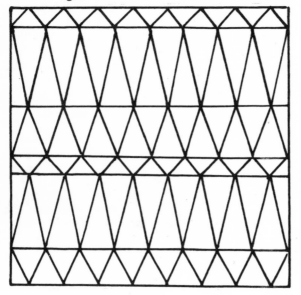

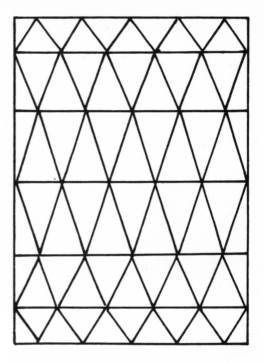

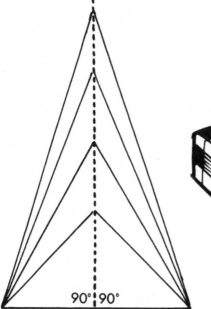

90° 90°

Ideas for footstool and pouffe

Beach bag and cushion

Made from towelling in long hexagons and squares this beach bag and cushion show two ways of making a pattern.

The cushion has a zip fastener, and the bag is lined with white PVC. The handles are of wood, enamelled white.

Beach bag and cushion in bright blues, greens, orange and yellow

Overleaf
Star panel, 66 cm x 43.2 cm (26 in. x 17 in.), by Alice Timmins. The star is of silver lurex fabric

Before Spring   Panel 40.6 cm x 76.2 cm (16 in. x 36 in.) by Alice Timmins
Irregularly shaped patches. See page 91

Shoulder bag

This is made from woollen tweeds in dark blues, greens, reds and browns. The patterns are made of *Vilene* or *Pellon* and are left in.

The bag is in continuous patchwork and is lined. Pockets may be made in the lining. The handle is a twisted woollen cord, sewn down the length of each side of the bag, and finished with a tassel.

Twisted cord

1 Wind about 23.8 m (26 yards) double knitting wool round two pencils held by two people facing each other about 3 m (2½ yards) apart. Diagram below.
2 Turn pencils in opposite directions until the strands are tightly twisted.
3 Suspend a small weight from the centre.
4 Bring the two pencils together and allow cord to twist.

One person alone can make a cord by substituting for pencils one cup hook on a wall and one in a brace (instead of a bit). By turning the handle of the brace the cord can quickly be twisted.

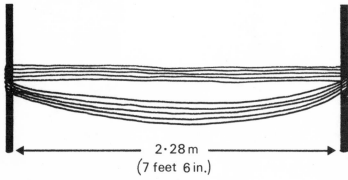

2·28 m
(7 feet 6 in.)

Tassels

1 Wind wool round card.
2 Pass thread through top, pull up and tie.
3 Cut wool at other end.
4 Tie thread tightly around about 19 mm ($\frac{3}{4}$ in.) from top. Pass ends into tassel.
5 Cover top with blanket stitch.

Stages in making a tassel

Overleaf
T for Temple Panel, 106.7 cm x 53.3 cm, by Marjorie Timmins. Square patches of different sizes (largest 7.6 cm (3 in.) fitted together. The many colours, strong contrasts of tone and the use of mostly patterned fabrics give the panel a great deal of vitality

Panel, 68.6 cm (27 in.) square, by Alice Timmins
5 cm (2 in.) squares in brown and greenish brown furnishing fabrics which are sewn to 7.6 cm (3 in.) squares in yellows and reds. These are in turn attached to a brownish yellow fabric background.
The patches were cut with turnings of a least 5 cm (2 in.) and were cross-tacked over (or could be stuck to) fairly thick card.
The small 5 cm (2 in.) card squares were covered first. These were stuck and, for complete safety, caught with stitches (worked from the back) to the larger squares of fabric. These in turn were used to cover the 7.6 cm (3 in.) cards which were, in the same way, fastened to the background fabric.
Care was taken to make sure that no turnings showed at the corners. Thick fabrics would make this difficult.

55

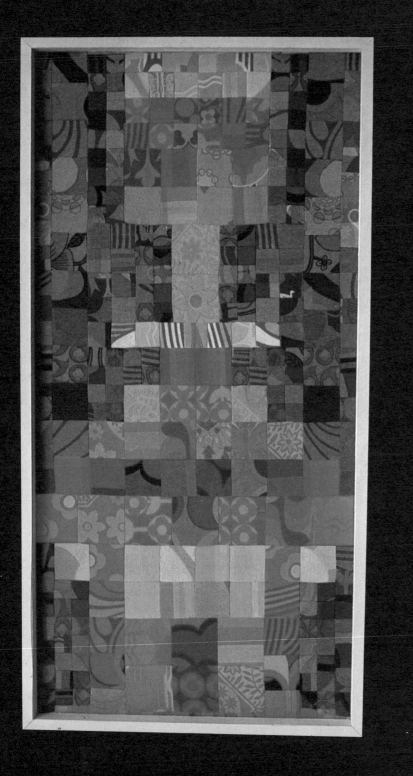

Dress

Many attractive and colourful garments can be made from patchwork. If a bought pattern is used, patches should be joined for each section separately, making sure that there is sufficient allowance for turnings The garment can then be cut out and made up.

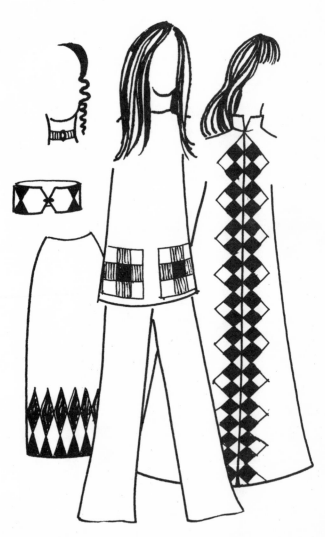

Patchwork for borders, pockets, belts and neckbands

Child's poncho by Maggie Norton. Made of triangular woollen patches sewn into strips which are joined with long bands. It has a woollen fringe

Patchwork coat in bright colours.
Hand-made by Jean Amsden

Overleaf
Skirt with motifs and border by Maggie Norton

Patchwork skirt by Maggie Norton. Design based on stained-glass windows

Smock

Triangular headscarf

Patchwork motifs applied on a smock by Suzy Ives

Triangular headscarf in pure silk. 15 cm (3 in.) squares in orange, pink and purple with darker squares in red and brown with some black. See page 89.

Evening bag

See page 65

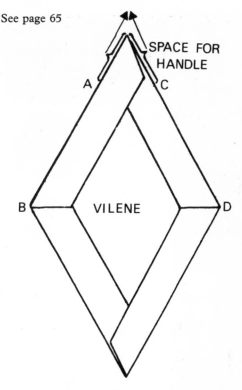

This is made from lurex fabrics in blue, purplish pink and silver, with several patches of white satin, machine embroidered with silk and gold lurex. Heavy weight *Vilene* or *Pellon* is used instead of paper for patterns.

Method

1. Sew 20 prepared patches and 2 half patches together to form the bag.
2. Make a silk lining to reach half way up the top patches – a turning at the top is advisable. Catch this in place.
3. With right sides together seam 6 extra patches to the top 6 patches, leaving enough space for handles at the top.
4. Turn these patches right side out, and slipstitch the two lower sides of the inner patches to the lining. This is done with the bag turned inside out.
5. Turn right side out and insert handles. Secure these with several stitches one over the other at the tips of the patches.
6. The handles may be made of string or piping cord covered with fabric, or two bangles of suitable colour.

Seam from A to B and from C to D

Evening bag in lurex fabrics made by Joyce Darby. The design was drawn first on paper. Method described on page 91

Overleaf
Panel 45.7 cm x 40.6 cm (18 in. x 16 in.). The light patches are cut from samples of linen furnishing fabric

Evening bag in lurex fabrics by Alice Timmins

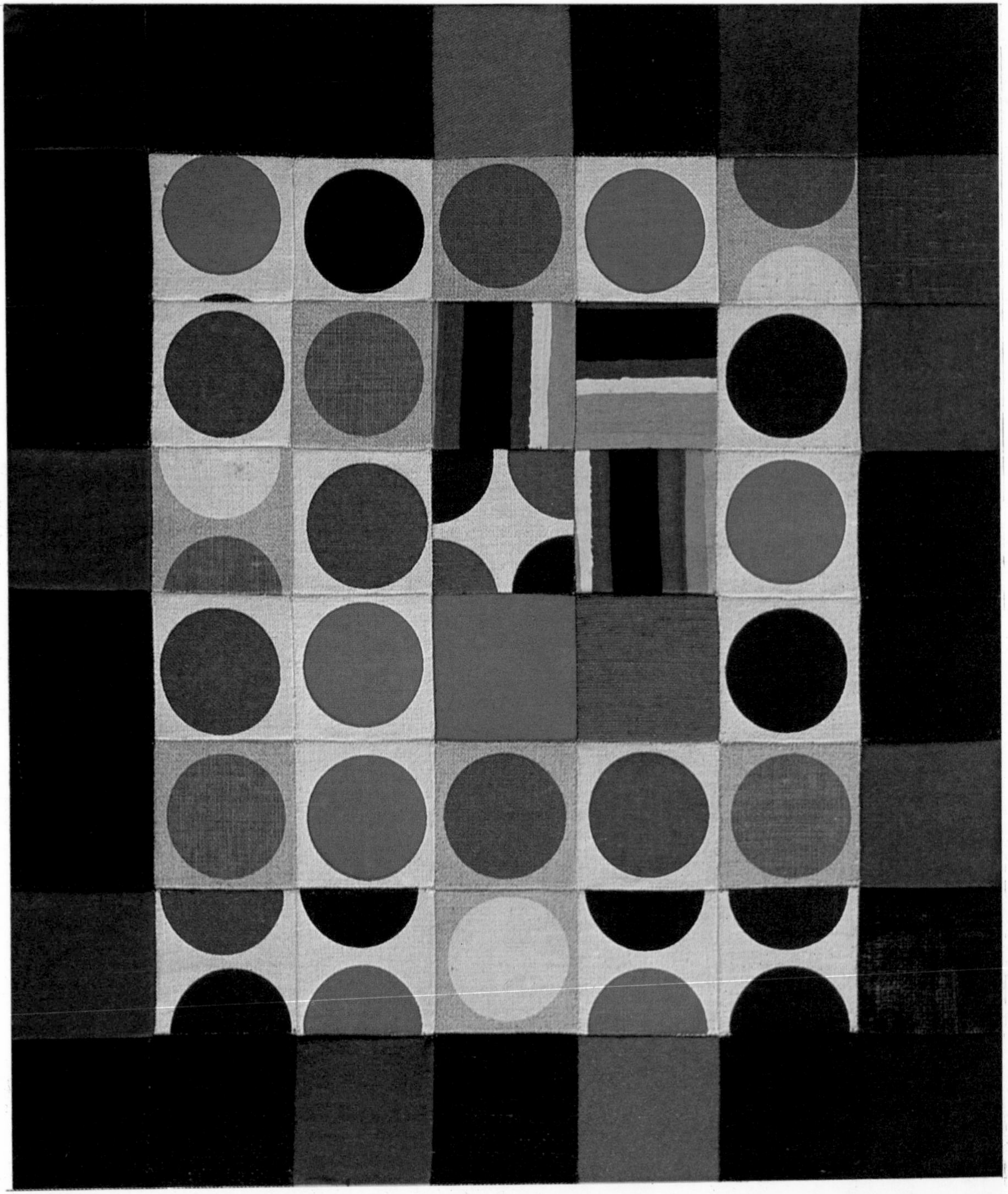

Bedcovers

When setting out to make a bedcover, the design should be thought out, and in some cases a scale drawing made.

It should be remembered that there are two different areas to be considered; the 'platform' or top of the bed, and the part which hangs over the sides. The design could emphasize the area of the platform, or could be an asymmetrical one on which the pattern may appear to fall over to the sides in places.

Some patchwork bedcovers have no definite pattern, the patches being arranged so that tones and colours make an attractive whole. A variation of tone could add interest; lightest patches in the centre and a gradual darkening to the outside, or vice versa.

A design may also be composed of motifs (page 71). They can be separated by arrangements of darker or lighter patches, but it will not improve the design if these patches are exactly alike, material having been bought for the purpose. Slight variations of colour or tone, or both, can add interest. In some cases a border may be added.

Another type of design has a large motif which fits the platform or top of the bed. It may be surrounded by smaller motifs and/or a border or borders.

Striped patterns with or without motifs between the stripes make all-over attractive designs.

Patchwork motifs may also be applied to a background fabric of suitable colour. A border made of patchwork could be added.

Cot cover by Jean Amsden. Hexagon and diamond patches in many bright colours form flowers which are separated by dark patches

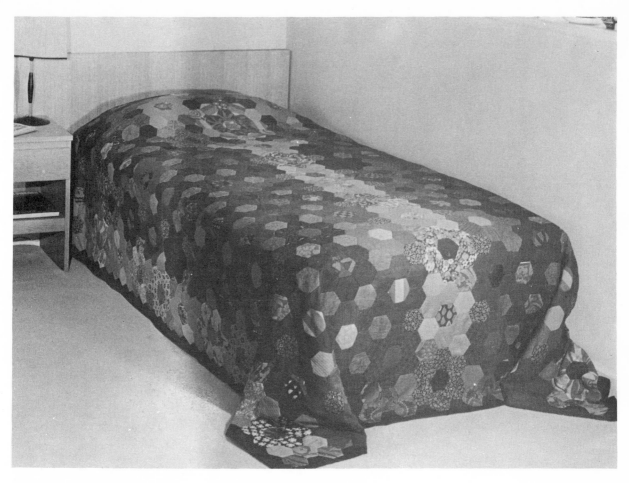

Single bedcover made by Annie Barnes. Dark patches are chiefly blues but some browns, purples and greys are introduced. The light hexagon flowers are bright greens and blues, both plain and patterned, with some reds. There is a border of similar hexagon flowers at each side

Overleaf
Patchwork used as a decoration on pillow slips by Suzy Ives. This idea can of course be extended for use on sheets   Photograph *Libra Studios*

Safari Machine made bedcover by Maggie Norton

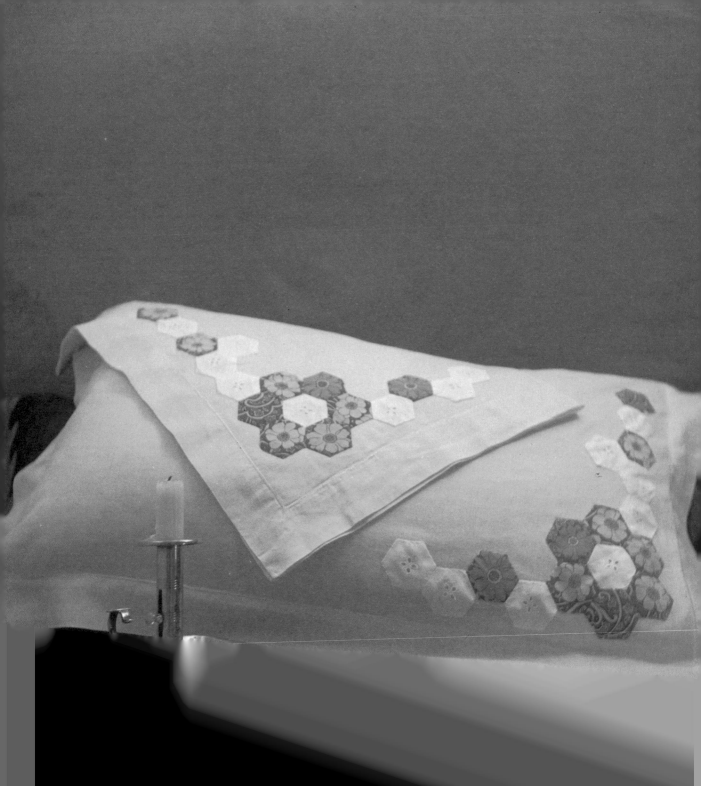

Finishing a bedcover

A firm but not heavy fabric should be used for lining.

The patchwork top, with edges trimmed, should be placed right side down on a flat surface. The lining should be carefully smoothed out on top, and the two pinned together at frequent intervals. A line of tacking about 25 mm (1 in.) in from the edge will make finishing the edges easier. At intervals of about 15.2 cm (6 in.) the lining and top must be caught together with several stitches one over the other.

The edges should meet exactly, and can then be finished with a binding, using a straight or bias strip. A piping could also be used. See page 46. In this case the lining is put on afterwards.

Another simple method is to turn in the edges of patchwork and lining so that the 15 mm ($\frac{1}{2}$ in.) turnings lie together inside. A row or two of running stitches close to the edge makes a firm finish.

If the patchwork top is rather small, it can be placed on a larger piece of lining fabric and invisibly hemmed to it. This means that the border (the edges of which can be bound) is part of the lining, so this should be of good quality, such as a smooth, firm furnishing fabric.

Alternatively, the larger lining could be folded over so as to cover the edges of the patches, and hemmed down on the right side. The corners should be mitred. See diagrams. Still another way is shown on page 29.

A fringe can in some cases make an attractive edging.

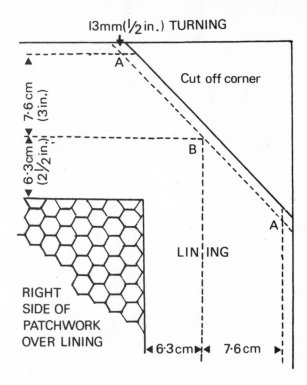

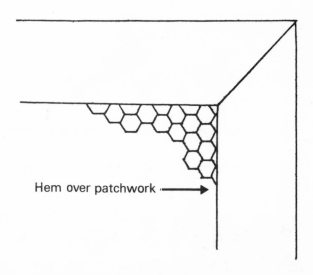

Bedcover by J. Bergh using 16 mm ($\frac{5}{8}$ in.) hexagons forming a crisp and pleasing design in diamond shapes. The cover is edged with a black fringe

Overleaf
Supermarket   Panel 40 cm x 118 cm (16 in. x 46 in.) by Alice Timmins 5 cm x 2 cm (2 in. x 2 in.) squares, with 5 cm x 25 mm and 5 cm x 15 m (2 in. x 1 in. and 2 in. x $\frac{1}{2}$ in.) rectangles. Many different types of cotton with some lurex fabrics were used. Traditional technique with patterns of heavy-weight *Vilene* left in

The early steps of a patchwork quilt being hand made by Frances Ross Duncan

Boxes

It is generally easier to make a box to fit the patch-work, but if a ready-made box is used, the size of template should be such that the patches at the edge are not cut off in a way which would spoil the design.

The thickness of the card used should be related to the size of the box. For the square box illustrated, 12.7 cm x 12.7 cm x 4.4 cm (5 in. x 5 in. x $1\frac{3}{4}$ in.), which is used as an example for methods A and B, mounting board 2 mm ($\frac{1}{16}$ in.) thick is suitable.

The turnings allowed at the outside edges of the patchwork should be at least 15 mm ($\frac{1}{2}$ in.) wide.

Method A

1 For lid and base cut 2 pieces of card 12.7 cm (5 in.) square and 4 pieces 12.7 cm x 4.4 cm (5 in. x $1\frac{3}{4}$ in.) for sides. Round off all edges with sandpaper.
2 *Lid* Stick a layer of wadding on one surface of the lid (2 mm larger than the lid on each side). Cut off excess at corners. Glue down the turnings of the prepared patchwork top over the padded lid, mitre the corners and ladder stitch them.
3 *For lining of lid* cut a 12.5 cm ($4\frac{7}{8}$ in.) square of heavyweight *Vilene* or *Pellon* or thin card. Cover this with lining fabric, sticking down the turnings on the underside. If card is used, a thin layer of wadding between card and lining will improve the appearance. Slipstitch this to underside of lid.
4 *For sides and base* cover as lid but cut the card or *Vilene* for lining 11.7 cm x 3.5 cm ($4\frac{3}{4}$ in. x $1\frac{3}{8}$ in.) for sides and 11.7 cm ($4\frac{3}{4}$ in.) square for base. Test before completing.
5 Seam the short sides together on wrong side.
6 Ladder stitch the fourth join, and ladder stitch sides to base.
7 Attach lid with buttonhole bars or fabric strips.
8 Stick a square of felt to the bottom of the box.

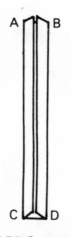

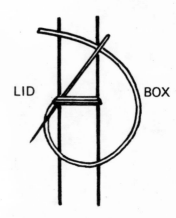

FABRIC HINGE

Fold AC to BD
Slipstitch together

Square box 12 cm x 12 cm x 3.8 cm (4¾ in. x 4¾ in. x 1½ in.)
Star shape in royal blue, green and blue-green shot silk.
Other patches in beige and light olive green. The tab is made from blue and
green beads
Oblong box 15 cm x 9.5 cm x 3.8 cm (6 in. x 3¾ in. x 1½ in.)
Made of browns, gold and silver with small patches in strong blues and greens.
The tab is an extension of an octagon patch

Overleaf
Box for necklaces, 25 cm x 7 cm x 5 cm (10 in. x 2¾ in. x 2 in.)
Trinket box, 15.2 cm x 6.4 cm x 3.2 cm (6 in. x 2½ in. x 1¼ in.)
Both box tops are made from strips of lurex fabrics
machined together. Designed and made by Alice Timmins

Workbox, 24 cm x 19 cm x 108 cm (9½ in. x 7½ in. x 4¼ in.), in lightweight furnishing fabrics. Hand made by Alice Timmins. The box is lined with royal blue
cotton poplin, and the lid has a border of the same fabric. Inside is a removable
tray with spaces for pincushion and needlecase

Method B

(Suitable for ready make box, in which case stages 1 and 2 below are omitted.)

1 Cut cards for lid, base and two sides as Method A but do not sandpaper them. The two other sides measure only 12.4 x 4.4 cm (4$\frac{7}{8}$ in. x 1$\frac{3}{4}$ in.)

2 Join sides and base with gummed paper strip or masking tape, with shorter sides placed as in the diagram.

3 *Lid* Pad, cover, and line as Method A, or line with felt over thin wadding.

4 *Sides* Stick a strip of wadding all round outer sides, wide enough to reach just over the top edges. Cut a strip of fabric 53.3 cm x 6.4 cm (21 in. x 2$\frac{3}{4}$ in.) and seam short ends together, so that it fits exactly round outside of box, with seam at one corner.
To reduce bulk, cut a small V 6 mm ($\frac{1}{4}$ in.) in depth at each corner (both top and base).

5 Stick the top edges over to the inside.

6 Stretching the fabric, stick the turnings over the base.

7 Lining – either of felt with thin wadding under, or of pieces of card or *Vilene* cut to fit exactly the sides and base inside the box, covered with fabric as Method A (4) and stuck in place.

8 Stick a square of felt over base.

Note Several variations are possible:
Edges may be piped.
Sides may also be of patchwork.
Large boxes (such as the workbox illustrated on page 77) should be made from thin plywood or hardboard.

Thin plastic foam, cotton or Terylene wadding may be used for padding. Heavy padding inside the box will serve no particular purpose and will reduce its capacity.

Fasteners and feet are often not necessary, but a small tab in front of the lid makes lifting the lid easy. This may in some cases be an extended patch.

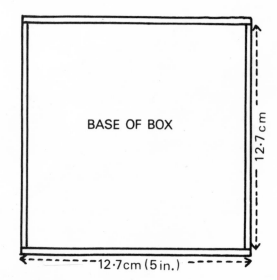

BASE OF BOX

12·7 cm

12·7cm (5 in.)

MITRE FOR BOX CORNERS

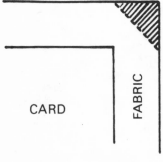

CARD

FABRIC

(a) Cut off shaded portion

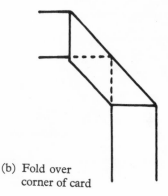

(b) Fold over corner of card

(c) Starting at arrow, ladder stitch to point and back again

EXPERIMENTS BASED ON TRADITIONAL TECHNIQUES

Overleaf
Floor cushion by Alice Timmins. This is a variation of traditional crazy patch-work in which small pieces of fabric were sewn to a cotton background with edges overlapping.

The work was started in the middle, unlike the traditional type in which the first patch was placed in a corner. The first ring of wedge-shaped patches was placed on a 68.6 cm (27 in.) square of firm cotton.

The next circle of patches was fitted underneath the first ring. This was repeated until the edges were reached.

The patches were pinned in place as the work proceeded (all edges overlapping by about 15 mm ($\frac{1}{2}$ in.)) and then were sewn down to the background fabric with fairly large hemming stitches (running stitch in traditional work). The hemming stitches were finally covered with herring bone stitch in red *Sylko Perlé* no. 5. The joins in the centre were covered with a 'spider's web' (see page 38). The cushion has a piped edge

Patchwork with irregular shapes See also pages 33, 48, 49 and 53

In this type of patchwork, where a template is not used, the work must be planned and drawn out first.

In a large piece of work, it will be found that the joins should generally pass completely from top to bottom and side to side, though not necessarily in straight lines. The slight thickness of the fabrics at the joins cause the patches to become fractionally larger, and this slight extra width must be distributed evenly. Otherwise the patches may have to be trimmed. Patterned or plain fabrics can be equally effective.

A drawing of the size of the finished work should be made first. This can be on paper, heavy weight *Vilene*, card, hardboard or plywood. A tracing of this serves as a guide. The original drawing is then cut up, and each piece covered with fabric, keeping the grain of the fabric in the same direction throughout. They are put in place on the tracing.

Patches with paper or *Vilene* patterns can be seamed together, or all types can be stuck to a rigid background.

Bedhead panel, 37 cm x 914 cm (36 in. x 17 in.), chiefly in purples, reds and pinks

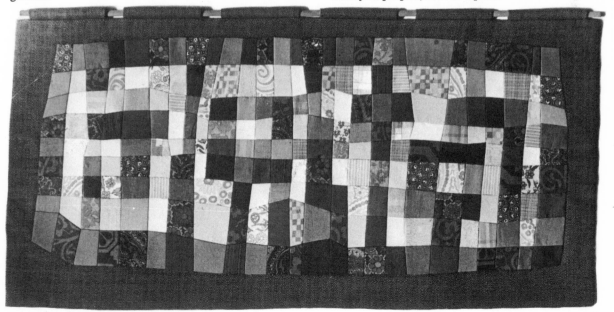

Patchwork project by second year students, Embroidery School, Faculty of Art and Design, Manchester Polytechnic. These panels show combinations of patchwork and appliqué. Irregularly shaped patches are seamed together and in some cases mounted on card. These are either sewn or stuck to the background See also colour plate page 49

Far right *It Grows Cooler*. Panel 127 cm x 30.5 cm (50 in. x 12 in.) by Alice Timmins. Freely cut squares in reds, orange and yellow, moving to cool greens and blues at the top, on a dark blue-green background. They are sewn down with herring-bone stitch in similar colours. There are some patches in gold and silver kid, sewn down with invisible nylon thread

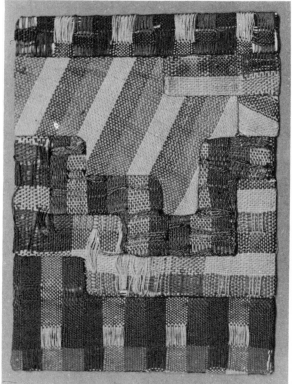

Panel made by Ros Ward. Cottons with printed and woven patterns, felt, artificial grass, braids, shisha glass, with some stitchery and dyed areas in the background

Pinholder

Cut two circles of paper or heavy-weight *Vilene* and two similar ones of thin card (diameter 8.9 cm (3½ in.)).

Divide one circle of paper with lines radiating from the centre. Cover each piece separately, tacking so that no stitches show on the right side, as the patterns are left in. Seam the sections together.

The back can be made in the same way, or may be plain.

Open out the turnings round the edge and with a running stitch gather each one over the circles of card.

Place top and underside together, right sides outside, and ladder stitch them together all round.

Pins are pushed in round the edges between the cards.

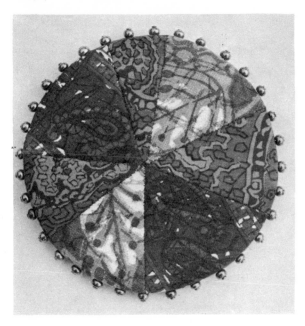

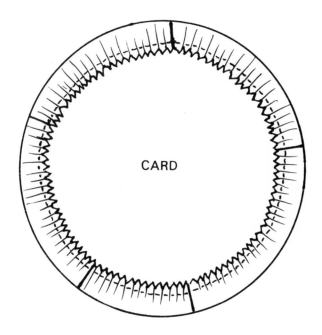

CARD

Details of an altar frontal made by Ruth Edmunds. Interlocking cardboard pieces are covered with felt, heavy cotton and crepe, with two background areas of corduroy. Some of the pieces were pintucked, others had wool or raffia couched on them

Patchwork appliqué with embroidery (by hand)

Altar Frontal in patchwork for Westminster Hospital Chapel by Beryl Dean
Mainly metallic fabrics with velvet.
Colours—gold, fawns, deep browns, purple, black, blues, reds and greens.
Applied shapes and couched copper and gold lurex passing enrich the patchwork

Experimental work by machine

See also pages 59 (poncho), 60, 61, 62 (headscarf), 69 and 76

Patches may in some cases be seamed together by machine. The shapes, however, must be simple, and rectangles are generally most suitable for this technique. Accuracy in cutting and sewing together the patches is necessary for a good result.

Method 1

Strips of varying widths can be seamed together to form long rectangles. Open out the turnings and press them flat, as shown in the diagram. Trim rectangles to size and join them with long narrow strips of fabric into a piece large enough for the required article.

Cushion in black and white with some red, royal blue and grey

Method 2

Squares or oblongs can be sewn together in various arrangements (See headscarf, page 62.)

Cut from metal or strong card a template the size of the finished patch. Place template on wrong side of fabric and mark round with pencil. Cut out the patch leaving 15 mm (½ in.) turnings. Repeat this as many times as necessary. Arrange the squares so as to make a satisfactory design, then pin them together in long strips. Machine sew along pencil lines. Press out seams. Pin and tack long sides of strips together, and machine, again along pencil lines. Press these seams before joining top to back.

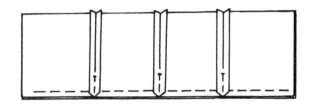

89

Method 3

A swing-needle machine is necessary for this method. The patches are ironed on to iron-on *Vilene*, and the joins covered with a wide zigzag stitch. The patches should overlap each other about 3 mm (⅛ in.). Calico can be used instead of *Vilene*.

Panel made by Judy Barry. Irregularly shaped patches on an iron-on *Vilene* base. Zigzag stitching on a *Bernina* Domestic sewing machine. Darker toned patches in blues and purples. Other patches in many colours

Method 4

The patches are cut exactly the same size as the chosen template. They are placed on iron-on *Vilene* with the edges meeting exactly, are pinned in place and carefully ironed down, a row at a time.

The joins are secured with wide zig-zag machine stitching with mercerised thread 30 to 35 stitches to 25 mm (1 in.). In this type of patchwork the article should be washed before being made up, to reduce stiffness.

Overleaf
Bedcover 7 m x 9 m (24 ft x 30 ft) made by Julia Roberts. Zigzag settings 3½ to 5 on *Singer* Domestic 211 sewing machine. Pinks and mauve to crimson and aubergine, and black and white with lime and sage greens. Appliqué panels machined in black; central lattice in white; other areas in pink

Method 3 Sampler
Centre—many strong bright colours. Background—dark greens and blues, growing lighter at the top

26873

Charlotte County Free Library
Charlotte Court House, Va.

Method 5

Patches may also be sewn with straight machine stitches to a suitable fabric background, using the latter as part of the design.

Crowded Beach, 48.5 cm x 94 cm (19 in. x 37 in.)
Squares and oblongs of brilliant colours are machined to a piece of bright yellow furnishing fabric. This is backed with strong calico to overcome the problem of puckering.
In the first stage only one side of each patch is sewn down.
The machined line is then taken diagonally to another patch, and so on until one side of each patch is secured. The process is repeated for the other three sides

Method 6

These diagrams show ways of combining methods 1 and 2 to make 30.5 cm (12 in.) blocks.

Seam together enough strips 33 cm (13 in.) long so as to make squares or blocks of 33 cm (13 in.) side. This allows 15 mm ($\frac{1}{2}$ in.) turnings. Blocks may of course, be larger or smaller than this. They can be joined as shown.

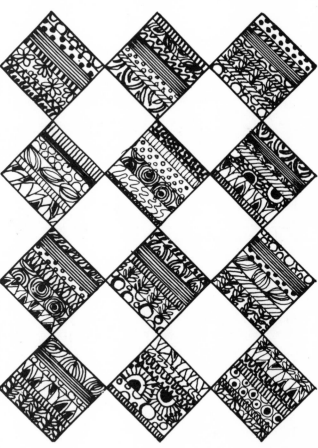

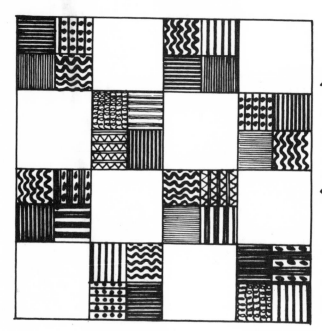

Method 7

Another method is to make the blocks from smaller squares and to place them diagonally or straight, alternating them with plain blocks.

Further reading

Introducing Patchwork
Alice Timmins, Batsford, London; Watson-Guptill
New York

Patchwork
Averil Colby, Batsford, London; Branford, Newton
Centre, Massachusetts

Old Patchwork Quilts and the Women who Made Them
Ruth E. Finlay, Lippincot, Philadelphia
Pennsylvania

American Quilts and Coverlets
Florence Peto, Parrish, London

Piet Mondrian
M. Seuphor, Thames and Hudson, London

Magic Squares
Paul Klee, Methuen, London

Applique Stitchery
Jean Ray Laury, Van Nostrand Reinhold, New York

Mosaics
P. B. Hetherington, Hamlyn, London

Mosaics
H.P. L'orange and P. J. Nordhagen, Methuen
London

Making Fabric Wall Hangings
Alice Timmins, Batsford, London; Branford
Newton Centre, Massachusetts

Curtains to Covers
Margaret Marchant, Evans, London

One Hundred and One Patchwork Patterns
Ruby McKim, Dover, New York

Stained Glass
Robert Sowers, Zwemmer, London

The Technique of Stained Glass
Patrick Reyntiens, Batsford, London; Watson-
Guptill, New York

Machine Embroidery: Technique and Design
Jennifer Gray, Batsford, London; Van Nostrand
Reinhold, New York

Suppliers

Great Britain

Templates
Mary Jackson
Churchtown
Southport, Lancashire

J. E. M. Patchwork Templates
Watlington, Oxfordshire, and
Forge House, 18 St Helen's Street
Cockermouth, Cumberland

The Needlewoman Shop
146–148 Regent Street
London W1

A. M. Row and Son Limited
42 Market Place
Ripon, Yorkshire

Vilene
Obtainable from most
department stores

Threads and embroidery accessories
E. J. Arnold (School Suppliers)
Butterley Street, Leeds LS10 1AX

Art Needlework Industries Ltd
7 St Michael's Mansions
Ship Street, Oxford

Craftsman's Mark Limited
Broadlands, Shortheath
Farnham, Surrey

Dryad
Northgates, Leicester

Hugh Griffiths
Brookdale, Beckington
Bath, Somerset

J Hyslop Bathgate and Company
Victoria Works, Galashiels

Mace and Nairn
89 Crane Street
Salisbury, Wiltshire

The Needlewoman Shop
146 Regent Street, London W1

Nottingham Handcraft Company
(School Suppliers)
Melton Road
West Bridgford, Nottingham

Christine Riley
53 Barclay Street, Stonehaven
Kincardineshire AB3 2AR

Suppliers in the USA

Threads and embroidery accessories
American Crewel Studio
Box 553 Westfield
New Jersey 07091

American Thread Corporation
90 Park Avenue, New York

Bucky King Embroideries Unlimited
121 South Drive,
Pittsburgh, Pennsylvania 15238

The Needle's Point Studio
1626 Macon Street, McLean
Virginia 22101

Yarncrafts Limited
3146 M Street
North West Washington DC

Pellon
Obtainable from most department stores

DATE DUE

NOV 21 79